Everyday Food

pasta

Joyce Bentley

Chrysalis Education

Distributed in the United States by
Smart Apple Media
2140 Howard Drive West
North Mankato, Minnesota 56003

ISBN 1-59389-221-7

Library of Congress control number: 2004108800

Senior editor: Rasha Elsaeed
Project editor: Debbie Foy
Editorial assistant: Camilla Lloyd
Food consultant: Brenda Alden
Art director: Sarah Goodwin
Illustrator: Molly Sage
Designer: Ben Ruocco, Tall Tree Ltd
Picture researchers: Sarah Stewart-Richardson, Veneta Bullen, Miguel Lamas

Printed in China

10 9 8 7 6 5 4 3 2 1

Words in **bold** can be found in Words to remember on page 30.

Picture Acknowledgements
All reasonable efforts have been made to ensure the reproduction of content has been done with the con-
sent of copyright owners. If you are aware of any unintentional omissions please contact the publishers
directly so that any necessary corrections may be made for future editions.

Anthony Blake Photo Library: Gerrit Buntrock 5, 14, John Sims 19B, Martin Brigdale 21, Eaglemoss Consumer
Publications 23T, Andrew Sydenham 23B; Image courtesy of The Advertising Archives: 7B; akg-images: Tony
Vaccaro 7T; Alamy Images: Gary Cook 19T; Alinari Archives, Florence: 6; Chrysalis Image Library: 10B, 12, Ray
Moller 24T, 24B, 25; Corbis: Owen Franken BC, 13T, Bohemian Nomad Picture 13B, 16, Vittoriano Rastelli 15T,
17, Baumgartner Olivia/SYGM 15B, Michael S. Yamashita 20, Julia Waterlow/Eye Ubiquitous 26; Cephas:
StockFood 10T; Empics: John Walton 27B; Frank Lane Picture Agency: Didier PRIX/Sunset 8, P Breson 9T, Roger
Wilmshurst 4; Pasta Reale Ltd: 18; PowerStock: Stuart Pearce 27T; Rex: Woman's Weekly 22; Royalty Free:
©Stockbyte FC, 1, 9B, 11

Contents

What is pasta?

Pasta is a type of food. Basic pasta is made from **durum wheat** flour and water. Sometimes egg or oil is added.

The **grains** of durum wheat are at the top of the plant. These are separated from the rest of the plant during **harvesting**.

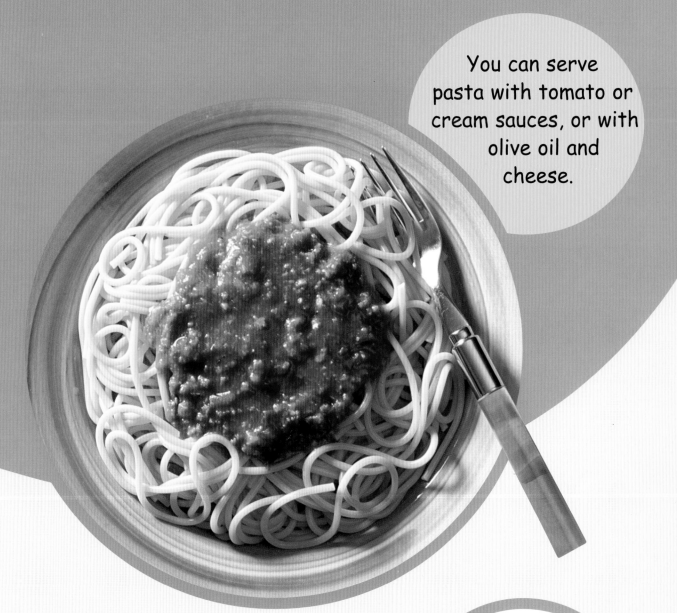

You can serve pasta with tomato or cream sauces, or with olive oil and cheese.

We usually eat pasta with sauces and fillings. These sauces can be made with vegetables, fish, or meat.

Across the world, there are over 600 different pasta shapes to choose from!

Back in time

It is thought that pasta was first discovered in China as long ago as 3,000 B.C. As **explorers** traveled the world, it was brought over to Italy and the rest of Europe.

These **medieval** women are preparing and drying pasta.

In Italy, pasta used to be dried on racks in the sun.

In 1789, Thomas Jefferson, who became President of the United States, brought the first pasta machine to the country. Pasta soon became popular.

This 1960s commercial shows a boy enjoying a bowl of spaghetti.

All kinds of pasta

When pasta is made, it is cut into shapes. There are many different shapes and sizes. These have Italian names such as ravioli, spaghetti, and cannelloni.

Tagliatelle is long, thin ribbons of pasta.

Fusilli means "little springs."

Spaghetti means "little strings."

These tiny pasta letters are often used in soups.

Macaroni is tube shapes of different lengths.

Farfelle means "butterflies."

Making pasta

Pasta flour is made from the inner part of the wheat grain. It is **ground** into a type of flour called **semolina**, then mixed with eggs and water to make a **dough**.

The dough ingredients are measured and often mixed on the table top.

The dough is **kneaded** by rolling and pressing it against a flat surface.

Pasta dough can also have tomato, **beet**, spinach, and other foods added to give it flavor and color.

Tricolore is a traditional pasta made with egg, tomato, and spinach. It is named after the red, white, and green of the Italian flag.

Shaping and drying pasta

The pasta dough is pushed through a machine with holes in it to give the pasta its shape.

Domestic pasta machines have attachments that can be used to make different pasta shapes.

The shape and size of the holes creates the various pasta shapes. The pasta is allowed to dry for up to two days, until it is **brittle** and ready for cooking or packing.

Squares of pasta are filled to make ravioli.

Noodles are made in factories. They are hung over racks to dry.

13

Cooking pasta

Pasta must be cooked before it is eaten. **Dried pasta** is cooked in boiling water until it is slightly soft. This is called **al dente.**

Dried pasta takes about 12 minutes to cook.

Fresh pasta cooks quickly in a few minutes. To make ravioli, the filling is cooked before being **sealed** into the pasta shapes.

A chef adds handfuls of fresh **herbs** to a tomato-based pasta sauce.

Fresh pasta is not allowed to dry. It is **sprinkled** with flour to stop it from sticking.

In the factory

Pasta is made in large quantities in a factory. The dough is made in containers called **vats**. Machines then shape the pasta.

Pasta dough is made into large, flat sheets before it is put through special machines that cut it into shape.

Strips of pasta are cut using sharp blades. It is dried by large driers that blow hot air at the pasta as it goes along the **conveyor belt**.

Pasta is packed into **airtight** packages to keep it fresh.

Getting to you

In the factory, the pasta is weighed and packed by machines before being loaded into crates. The information on the package tells us how to cook the pasta, what it weighs, and how to store it.

Trucks travel across the country to deliver pasta to shops.

Italian dried pasta comes in a variety of shapes and colors.

You can buy pasta in packages in the supermarket. A special shop called a **delicatessen** sells fresh pasta and **imported** Italian dried pasta.

Fresh pasta is often made in delicatessens and sold the same day.

Eating pasta

There are many ways to serve pasta. Most pasta is eaten with a tomato, cream, or herb sauce. You can add cheese, vegetables, meat, or fish to pasta dishes.

Lasagne is made with pasta sheets and layers of ground beef, tomatoes, and cream sauce.

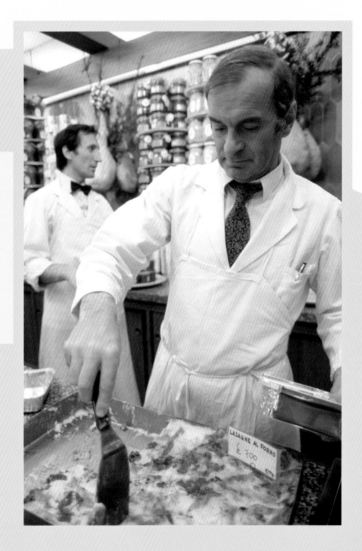

Pasta can also be put into salads, casseroles, and soups. In Italy, it is eaten with just a little sauce to cover it.

The Italians name their pasta after its shape. For example, vermicelli means "little worms" and conchiglie means "shells."

Pesto sauce is a very popular sauce for pasta. It is made from olive oil, basil, and **pine nuts**.

Everyone loves pasta

Pasta is enjoyed around the world. It forms part of a **staple diet** for many people as it is cheap and easy to find.

This Japanese dish is called ramen. It is a soup made with egg noodles, meat or fish, and vegetables.

The Chinese eat lots of noodles. These have been fried to make them crispy.

Many countries have their own special pasta recipes made with locally grown **produce**.

Linguini is thin ribbons of pasta. Here it is cooked with chicken, pesto sauce, and **Parmesan** cheese.

A balanced diet

Pasta is a **carbohydrate**, which comes from the wheat grain used to make the flour. Pasta made with egg contains **protein,** and **whole wheat** pasta is a good source of **fiber**.

Other carbohydrates include potatoes, bread, and rice.

Fruit and vegetables contain carbohydrates and provide lots of **vitamins** and fiber.

For a balanced diet, most of the food we eat should come from the groups at the bottom of the chart and less from the top.

Fat, oils, and sweets group

Milk group

Meat group, including fish, nuts, and eggs

Vegetable group

Fruit group

Grain group, including potatoes

Healthy pasta

The carbohydrates in pasta give us energy. People who lead active lives need more carbohydrates than those who are less active.

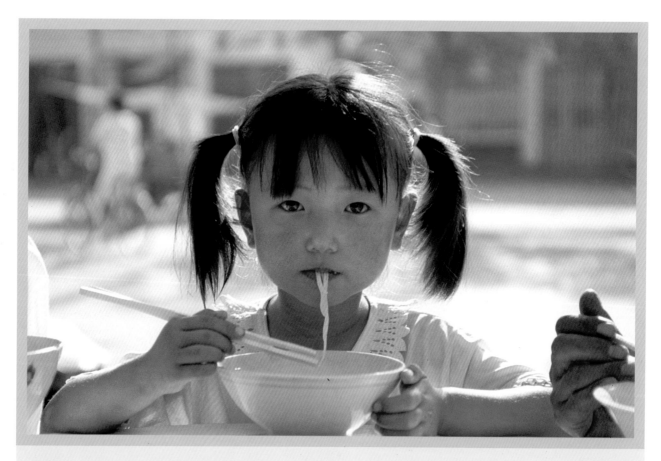

The protein in egg noodles helps us to grow and stay healthy.

Children use up lots of energy when they are playing, so they need plenty of carbohydrates.

Pasta is good for athletes because it releases energy over a long period of time.

Pasta salad

This colorful dish tastes great on its own or eaten with garlic bread.
Serves 2

Children in the kitchen must be supervised at all times by an adult.

YOU WILL NEED

- 2 cups (4 oz) cooked, cooled pasta shapes
- 4 cherry tomatoes
- 1-in (2 cm) piece cucumber
- ½ cup (3 oz) cheese
- Olive oil
- Black pepper

1. Chop the cucumber and cheese into cubes.

2. Cut the tomatoes in half.

3. Mix the pasta and other ingredients in a bowl and pour a little olive oil over it.

4. Add some black pepper and serve!

Words to remember

airtight No air can get in or out.

al dente Cooked until firm to the bite.

beet Round, purple root vegetable.

brittle Hard but breaks easily.

carbohydrate A nutrient the body needs for energy.

conveyor belt Machine that carries things from one place to another.

delicatessen Shop that sells meats, cheeses, and imported foods.

domestic Things that are made for the home.

dough A flour and water mixture, sometimes also with egg.

dried pasta Pasta that has been allowed to dry thoroughly.

durum wheat A kind of plant. The wheat grains are crushed to make flour.

explorers People who travel in search of new places.

fiber Material found in some foods that helps digestion.

fresh pasta Pasta that has not been allowed to dry.

grain The seeds at the top of a cereal plant.

ground To crush something into a powder.

harvesting Pulling crops from the ground when they are ready to eat.

herbs Plants that are used to flavor food.

imported To bring food in from another country to sell.

kneaded To squeeze and press dough to soften it.

medieval A time in history between the fifth and fifteenth centuries.

Parmesan Hard, dry cheese often sprinkled on top of pasta.

pine nuts The edible seeds of some pine trees.

protein A nutrient that is necessary for growth and repair.

produce Food that is made to sell.

sealed To fasten something so that nothing gets in or out.

semolina Flour that is made from grinding durum wheat grains.

sprinkled To scatter over something.

staple diet Food that forms the main part of the diet.

tricolore The flag of Italy, which is red, green, and white.

vats Large containers used in factories.

vitamins Nutrients we need for health and to prevent sickness.

whole wheat Pasta made from flour that uses the whole grain.

Index